'A wonderful gift and legacy  ly
and freshly written. This is o   ul
books on leadership for matι   ;
and challenges. It's a balanced blend of solid and grounded
biblical foundation, personal examples and deep pastoral insights,
relevant and contextual application. It will enrich every servant
leader whose aspiration is to lead like Jesus, with humility,
integrity, sacrifice and by example.'
*Dr Daniel Bourdanné, General Secretary of the International
Fellowship of Evangelical Students (IFES)*

'As I read this short but powerful book by John Stott, I was
reminded of the impact of the lectures that he presented in Quito,
Ecuador, in 1985. They touched my life at a crucial point as we
experienced a change of leadership in evangelical student work in
Latin America. Since I met him in Cambridge in 1959, Stott had
modelled for me a truly biblical style of leadership. I know hundreds
of people around the world who have had the same experience. In
these chapters you will find biblical exposition, personal examples
and fascinating anecdotes that reflect the principles that explain
why he kept his successful leadership role in world evangelicalism.
He uses a clear and attractive narrative style that makes for easy
reading but always takes you to a reflective mood.'
*Samuel Escobar, past president of the International Fellowship of
Evangelical Students*

'John Stott was a leader who never stopped learning. His posture
of humility before God, before the Scriptures, before friends and
even before enemies was one of his most remarkable traits. This
set of lectures captures some of this spirit in a plain and
compassionate way. For a leader who seeks humble courage, it
can be tasted in this word of witness from one who lived it to the
glory of the Lord he followed.'
Mark Labberton, president of Fuller Theological Seminary, author of
The Dangerous Act of Loving Your Neighbor

Challenges of Christian Leadership

JOHN STOTT

Challenges of Christian Leadership

ivp

INTER-VARSITY PRESS
Norton Street, Nottingham NG7 3HR, England
Email: ivp@ivpbooks.com
Website: www.ivpbooks.com

Originally published in Spanish in Argentina under the title *Desafíos del Liderazgo Cristiano*. Published in the United States of America by InterVarsity Press, Downers Grove, Illinois.

Unless otherwise stated, Scripture quotations are taken from the Holy Bible, New International Version® Anglicized, NIV® Copyright© 1979, 1984, 2011 by Biblica, Inc.® Used by permission. All rights reserved worldwide.

Scripture quotations marked KJV are from the King James (Authorized) Version.

The Scripture quotation marked NASB is from the New American Standard Bible®, Copyright © 1960, 1962, 1963, 1968, 1971, 1972, 1973, 1975, 1977, 1995 by The Lockman Foundation. Used by permission.

Material in chapter 5 is excerpted from *John Stott: A Portrait by His Friends*, edited by Christopher J. H. Wright (IVP, 2011). Used by permission.

First published 2014

British Library Cataloguing in Publication Data
A catalogue record for this book is available from the British Library

ISBN: 978–1–78359–088–9

Typeset by CRB Associates, Potterhanworth, Lincolnshire
Printed and bound in Great Britain by Ashford Colour Press Ltd, Gosport, Hampshire

Inter-Varsity Press publishes Christian books that are true to the Bible and that communicate the gospel, develop discipleship and strengthen the church for its mission in the world.

Inter-Varsity Press is closely linked with the Universities and Colleges Christian Fellowship, a student movement connecting Christian Unions in universities and colleges throughout Great Britain, and a member movement of the International Fellowship of Evangelical Students. Website: www.uccf.org.uk

CONTENTS

FOREWORD

As a young person, I learned many lessons about the lifestyle of a leader through the life and writings of John Stott. It is amazing how many of those lessons I am still using after almost four decades of ministry. This book has many such lessons that a young Christian leader can glean to help him or her become a biblical leader.

I read this book slowly as a part of my devotional reading. As few books have done to me, I found my heart burning with things God was teaching me as I read. Often I had to stop to pray. There are challenges to leaders about commitment to Christ, to people, to personal discipline, and to several other things that make people good leaders. There is also much wisdom on how one leads effectively.

I am surprised that such a helpful book is being published so many years after the messages it contains were originally given. But, as they say, better late than never!

Ajith Fernando
Teaching Director, Youth for Christ
Author of *Jesus Driven Ministry*

PREFACE

This book is drawn from four talks given by John Stott in 1985 in Quito, Ecuador, at a conference for the staff of International Fellowship of Evangelical Students (IFES) movements in Latin America. This material was first published in Spanish as *Desafíos del Liderazgo Cristiano* (Ediciones Certeza), but has not previously been published in English.

The material was drawn to our attention by Doug Stewart, formerly an IFES staffworker in Bolivia, Argentina and Mexico from 1964 to 1991, and now a vice-president for IFES. Doug served as John Stott's translator at the 1985 Quito conference. He recently came across his transcripts of the talks and offered them to us to be published. We are pleased to make this timeless treasure available in English.

John Stott began with some personal remarks to introduce this series:

I would like to say what a great privilege it is for me to spend these four afternoons with you, because I want to begin by saying how strongly committed I am to the IFES. My involvement began forty-five years ago when I went up to Cambridge as a student. I was going into what used to be called the CICCU, now usually known as the Christian Union.

Then from 1952 to 1977, which is twenty-five years, I had the joy of leading university missions in many countries of the world, in Europe and North America, in Africa and Asia and Australia. I've often spoken to many student conferences in many parts of the world, so I've been given a wonderful chance to observe IFES closely. I tell you honestly, I'm deeply grateful to God for it. I'm grateful for the principles on which it operates: national indigenous movements, student leadership, thoughtful evangelism and mature discipleship. I'm also grateful for the quality of leadership that God has given the movement, both in staff and in students. That includes yourselves, whom it has been a joy for me to meet these weeks. So thank you for the chance to spend these four afternoons with you.

I've been asked to share with you both from the Scriptures and from experience, but to do so a little more informally. Now may I tell you the four topics that I have chosen under the general heading of 'Challenges of Christian Leadership'. One challenge is discouragement, or how to persevere under pressure. Two, the challenge of self-discipline, or how to maintain spiritual freshness. Third is the challenge of relationships, or how to treat people with respect. Fourth, the challenge of youth, or how to be a leader when still comparatively young.

We do not lose heart.

Chapter 1

THE CHALLENGE OF
DISCOURAGEMENT

How to persevere under pressure

The pressures on Christian leaders are intense and often unrelenting. Let's think of some of them. There are our busyness and fatigue, with inadequate time for the family, not even for holidays. Then there are the responsibilities that recognized leaders have. If their ministry is criticized, they bear the brunt of the criticism, and they have the responsibility of making difficult decisions.

There are also the disappointments of the work. Promising potential leaders do not always live up to their promise. Some even fall away. Promising ministries begin to decline in numbers or in vision, and that is a great disappointment to the leader. In addition, there are the personal temptations with which the devil attacks all leaders, and there is the loneliness that we experience at the top. We may have no peers in whom to confide.

All these problems can lead us into discouragement. In fact, discouragement is the greatest occupational hazard of a believer, as it can lead to loss of vision and enthusiasm. So the question is how to persevere under these pressures.

I'd like us to turn to 2 Corinthians 4, and I hope you won't mind if I give a little Greek lesson. The first verse reads, 'Therefore, since through God's mercy we have this ministry, we do not lose heart.' And then verse 16 says, 'Therefore we do not lose heart. Though outwardly we are wasting away, yet inwardly we are being renewed day by day.'

Notice the phrase that is repeated in these two verses: *ouk enkakoumen.* That is the Greek phrase that comes in verse 1 and verse 16. Most modern English versions say, 'We do not lose heart.' Another is: 'We refuse to become dispirited', or 'Nothing can bother us.' There is a similar expression that comes to mind in chapter 5 to which I'd draw your attention: 'Therefore we are always confident' (verse 6), and again, 'We are confident, I say' (verse 8). That means we are of good courage.

You may know these chapters well enough to know that in chapter 3 Paul unfolds the glory of the Christian ministry, but in chapter 4 he unfolds the problems of the Christian ministry. This is his argument: because of the glory of the ministry and in spite of its problems, *ouk enkakoumen.* We refuse to become discouraged.

Two problems: the veil and the body

There are two questions before us: what problems tempted Paul to lose heart? And second, what solutions or antidotes did he find to them? There are two problems that caused discouragement in this chapter. The first is an external and objective problem in our listeners, and the second is an internal and subjective problem in ourselves.

The first he calls the veiling, which is *kalyma*. This is the veil that lies over the minds of unbelievers, and it blinds them to the truth of the gospel. The second is *soma*, the body. That is our own body, its frailty, this fragile human vessel, which maintains the treasure of the gospel.

So the first problem is *spiritual*: it is the blindness of the people we preach to. The second is *physical*: it is our personal fragility and mortality. When you have a weak preacher and a blind congregation, you have a problem on your hands. These are the two problems, and I do not think there is anything that causes more discouragement than these.

Where is the veil? Look at 2 Corinthians 3:12: 'Since we have such a hope, we are very bold. We are not like Moses, who would put a veil over his face.' In other words, the veil in the people's minds is not our doing. On the contrary, we are very bold in our preaching and we set forth the truth plainly. Therefore, the cause of this human blindness is diabolical; it affects both Jews and Gentiles. Look on to chapter 3 verse 14. In the middle of the verse: 'for to this day the same veil remains when the old covenant is read'.

Again, verse 15: 'Even to this day when Moses is read, a veil covers their hearts.' So twice Paul says it for emphasis: the Jews have a veil over their minds and hearts. Then Paul goes on to say, so do the Gentiles. Chapter 4 verse 4: 'The god of this age has blinded the minds of unbelievers.'

Now think with me, is this not one of our major problems? We make the gospel crystal clear, but people cannot grasp it. We spell it out so simply that we think even a child could understand it, but they don't. We explain it, we argue it, we plead with people until we think they are bound to yield, but a veil lies over their minds. I doubt if there is anything more discouraging than that to the Christian worker. It can lead to great frustration. So (a) the first problem is the veil, which we'll come back to in a minute when we think of the solutions to the problems, and (b) is the body.

Paul writes about the body in 2 Corinthians 4:7–18. Verse 7: 'we have this treasure in jars of clay' – that is, as in an old-fashioned oil lamp, so in the Christian worker, there is a contrast between the treasure and its container. There's no doubt that Paul is referring to our physical frailty in which we hold the gospel. Written all over the human body are the words 'fragile: handle with care'. The immediate reference is to his persecution, which is clear from verses 8 and 9, but it refers to this weakness in other contexts. In 1 Corinthians 2:3 he says, 'I came to you in weakness and fear, and with much trembling.' The weakness seems to be more psychological than physical: it was his natural nervousness when going to Corinth with the gospel. Then the third example in 2 Corinthians 12:7 where he referred to his 'thorn in the flesh': 'To keep me from becoming conceited [because of these surpassingly great revelations], there was given me a thorn in the flesh, a messenger of Satan, to torment me . . . and [Jesus] said to me, "My grace is sufficient for you, for my power is made perfect in weakness."'

Paul goes on in verse 10 to refer to weaknesses, insults, hardships, persecutions and difficulties, so it seems once again that this is a physical disability. It may have been a sickness or a disability of some kind. We can probably add frailties of our own to this list. You may have the shyness of an introvert, the liability to depression, or you may have headaches. All these are examples of the weakness of the human body. It is the

We do not lose heart.

weakness of the container, which holds the treasure of the gospel.

Here are two major problems that we cannot handle by ourselves. We cannot lift the veil, we cannot cure the blindness of unbelievers, and we cannot overcome the frailty of our own minds and bodies. Yet it is in spite of these apparently insuperable problems that Paul says *ouk enkakoumen*. We do not lose heart. How then can we overcome this discouragement when we are faced with these problems?

The antidote to discouragement

Let us turn secondly from the problems to the antidotes to discouragement. Rather, I think we should say 'antidote' in the singular, for although there are two problems, there is only one solution: the power of God. Let's look again at the veil and the body.

First, the veil. What do we do when people refuse to respond to the gospel? Well, you know what our temptation is. We are tempted to force them to do it. We are tempted to resort to emotional and psychological techniques to manipulate people into believing, or to manipulate the gospel to make it easier to believe.

But although the temptation to some kind of manipulation is very strong when people don't believe, Paul specifically renounces that temptation. 2 Corinthians 4:2: 'Rather, we have renounced secret and shameful ways; we do not use deception, nor do we distort the word of God. On the contrary, by setting forth the truth plainly we commend ourselves to every man's conscience.' You reject manipulation, but on the contrary make the plain proclamation of the gospel.

Now read 2 Corinthians 4:4, 6: 'The god of this age has blinded the minds of unbelievers, so that they cannot see the light of the gospel of the glory of Christ, who is the image of God.' 'For God, who said, "Let light shine out of darkness," made his light shine in our hearts to give us the light of the knowledge of the glory of God in the face of Christ.' I think these are very important verses for us to understand. In verse 6 Paul is referring back to Genesis 1:2–3. He likens the unregenerate heart to the primeval chaos, when everything was formless and empty and dark until God said, 'Let there be light', and light shone into the darkness. There is Paul's picture of regeneration. This is what happened to him on the Damascus Road. The God who in Genesis said, 'Let there be light', has shone in our hearts. Thus regeneration is nothing less than a new creation of God, and it does not take place until God says, 'Let there be light.'

Here we have two gods in conflict with each other. In verse 4 Satan is called 'the god of this age'; in verse 6 Paul speaks of the God of creation. The god of this age blinds people's eyes, their minds, while the God of creation shines into their hearts. There is a complete and absolute contrast between them. One god is blinding and the other is shining. What then can we hope to contribute to this conflict? Would it not be modest and wise perhaps to retire from the scene of conflict? Shall we not let these two gods fight it out?

But no, Paul's conclusion is a different one. Look at verse 5: 'For we do not preach ourselves, but Jesus Christ as Lord, and ourselves as your servants for Jesus' sake.' You see, the battle between God and the devil concerns the light. The devil seeks to stop the light from shining, but if God is causing the light to shine, what is this light? It's important to notice that it is the gospel. Look at the end of verse 4: 'the light of the gospel of the glory of Christ, who is the image of God', and the end of verse 6: 'the knowledge of the glory of God'. So the gospel is the light. It is the means by which God overcomes the darkness and shines into people's hearts.

So if the gospel is the light, we'd better preach the gospel. Far from being unnecessary, evangelism is absolutely indispensable. Preaching of the gospel is the God-appointed means by which the prince of darkness is overthrown and by which God shines into people's hearts. So *ouk enkakoumen*. We do not lose heart. The veil is there over people's minds. We cannot penetrate it by our own power, but it can be penetrated by the power of God when the gospel is preached.

God's power in weakness

Let me move to the final point, the second problem, the body. I want to look at the three Corinthian verses we looked at before. We begin with 2 Corinthians 4:7: 'We have this treasure in jars of clay to show that this all-surpassing power is from God and not from us.' Just note that 'to' ('in order that').

Second, turn back to 1 Corinthians 2:3–5: 'I came to you in weakness and fear, and with much trembling. My message and my preaching were not with wise and persuasive words, but with a demonstration of the Spirit's power' (and again 'in order that') 'so that your faith might not rest on men's wisdom, but on God's power'.

The third one is 2 Corinthians 12:7: 'There was given me a thorn in my flesh', which Jesus declined to take away from him. So Paul says in verse 9, 'I will boast . . . about my weaknesses', and again we have 'in order that', 'so that Christ's power may rest on me'. Three times Paul uses this phrase 'in order that', and I cannot think that it is an accident. This is the emphasis of the Corinthians' correspondence: that God's power is demonstrated in human weakness and that God's might is manifested through death.

Back to our text in 2 Corinthians 4, let's look at verses 10 and 12: 'We always carry around in our body the death of Jesus, so that the life of Jesus may also be revealed in our body . . . So then, death is at work in us, but life is at work in you.' See, we are carrying about in our bodies the dying of Jesus, so that the life of Jesus may be manifest in our mortal flesh. Power through weakness and life through death is the theme of these two letters.

What then do we do if we feel this weakness of our mortal flesh? Like Paul, we pray that we may be delivered from a thorn in the flesh, and God may deliver us. Our headaches may pass, our physical infirmities may be healed, our psychological shyness may be taken away from us, but they may not. I believe that Scripture and experience both teach this rather unpalatable lesson: that God often deliberately keeps us in weakness in order that his power may rest upon us.

A personal example

Before I conclude, I would like to take the liberty of sharing one personal experience with you. It was during a mission at the University of Sydney in Australia in 1958. During the week of the convention I had caught what we call a 'bug', and I lost my voice. What can you do with a missionary who has no voice?

We had come to the last night of the mission, the eighth night. The students had booked the big university hall and a large number of students came. It was agreed that I would attempt to preach. I was sitting in a little room just outside the university hall. A group of students gathered around me, and I asked them to read this passage in 2 Corinthians 12. We prayed that the thorn in the flesh might be taken away from me, and if I remember rightly they laid hands on me with prayer. But we went on to pray that if it pleased God to keep me in weakness, I would rejoice in my infirmities in order that the power of Christ might rest upon me, because when I am weak I am strong.

I remember that I had to get within one inch of the microphone. I croaked the gospel. I was unable to use any inflections of voice, was unable to express personality. I was just a croak in a monotone, and all the time we were crying to God that his power would be demonstrated in human weakness. It would be tempting for me to exaggerate or to be dishonest, but I can honestly say that there was a far greater response that night than every other night.

What encourages me much more is the following. Since 1958, I've been back to Australia about ten times, and on every occasion some body has come up to me and said, 'Do you remember that night of preaching in the university hall when you'd lost your voice?' and I'd say, 'How could I ever forget it?' And the person responded, 'I was converted that night.' It has been a great illustration of this principle to me, that God's power is demonstrated in human weakness.

Let me sum up what we've tried to learn together. The veil over people's minds is very thick. Our body is very frail. But it is not beyond the power of God either to penetrate the veil or to sustain the body, so *ouk enkakoumen*. We do not lose heart, and that is perfectly clear even against these pressures.

I finish with yet another Australian illustration about perseverance. Thomas Sutcliffe Mort was an early British settler in Sydney. Some of the docks in Sydney are named after him. At the beginning of the nineteenth century he set himself the task of solving the problem of refrigeration. They were exporting meat from Australia to Europe, but it all went bad before it arrived. So Thomas Mort determined to invent an effective method of

To persevere is to succeed.

refrigeration. He gave himself three years in which to do it, but it took him twenty-six. He lived long enough to see the first consignment of refrigerated meat leave Australia, but he died before it arrived.

Written all around his study is his motto. I happen to know about it because his house is now occupied by the Archbishop of Sydney. Round the top of the wall he's written his motto twenty times: to persevere is to succeed. So God give us grace to persevere. *Ouk enkakoumen.*

I believe that indiscipline is often at the root of staleness.

Chapter 2

THE CHALLENGE OF
SELF-DISCIPLINE

How to maintain spiritual freshness

I want to talk about the challenge of self-discipline and how to maintain our spiritual freshness. The problem is not so much discouragement as staleness, another very common problem of Christian leaders. It is easy for our vision to begin to fade and even our faith to grow small. The glory of the gospel can become tarnished so that it no longer excites us. The sparkle goes out of our eyes, the spring goes out of our steps, and we begin to look like stagnant pools instead of like running streams.

So here is our second problem: in the midst of all the pressures that are upon us, how can we not only overcome discouragement but maintain spiritual freshness? I have no one passage of Scripture to bring, but would like to talk from experience as well as from Scripture. In general, I want to say that I am an impenitent believer in the importance of discipline. I believe that indiscipline is often at the root of staleness.

The discipline of rest and relaxation

Let me talk about three kinds of discipline. The first I'm going to call the discipline of rest and relaxation. We are extremely psychosomatic creatures. In fact, we are pneumato-psychosomatic creatures, because we are body, mind and spirit. We do not find it easy to understand the interrelation between these three, but we know that the condition of any one affects the others. Especially, the condition of our body affects our spiritual life. Sometimes people come to me with a spiritual problem, and I know the solution to their spiritual problem is to take a week's vacation. When we're tired or sick, we don't feel like reading the Scriptures. We don't feel like praying. We don't feel like witnessing to Jesus Christ. But when we feel better physically, then these things are easy. So here are some aspects of the discipline of rest.

> *I believe that indiscipline is often at the root of staleness.*

First is *the need to take time off.* Some Christian leaders are compulsive workers. They are overscrupulous, and they think there is something wrong if they are not working morning, noon and night. They claim Jesus as their patron, saying that Jesus was available to anybody at any time, but their knowledge of the Bible leaves much to be desired. Jesus was not available all the time. The text I would like to give compulsive workers is Mark 6:45: 'Immediately Jesus made his disciples get into the boat and go on ahead of him to Bethsaida, while he dismissed the crowd.' He dismissed the crowd in order to go away and rest and pray, so we must not feel guilty if we are taking a period of rest.

I myself am very thankful for the afternoon siesta. I could not get up early in the morning if it wasn't for the afternoon siesta. I remember very well my first visit to Latin America. I'd been right around the continent, and I was to leave from Argentina. It was my last night in Buenos Aires and somebody asked in the public meeting if I had learned anything while I was in Latin America. I was able to reply at once that I had learned three valuable lessons. The first was the great benefit of the afternoon siesta, the second was to repent of my particularly English vice of punctuality, and the third was to have liberty to kiss everybody within reach. I added that I would have to forget two of those lessons before I got back to London. I left them to guess which, but you will guess that it is the siesta that I have continued. So we do need adequate sleep, and of course our need varies according to our temperament. We also need to take time off to rest during the day as well as at night.

I hope those of you who are married give adequate time to your family. I've always admired my successor as rector of All Souls. His name is Michael Baughen, and he is a wonderful family man. He and his wife are very happy, and they have three grown-up children, a fine example of Christian family life. Michael made a rule that he would always have the evening meal with his family. This was when the children were small and they had their meals fairly early, at perhaps 5:30 or 6:00. But no matter how important the business was, he would leave to have a meal with his family. The balancing was good. He had taken on this responsibility and he had to keep it.

We ought to take a day off every week. I'm afraid I am rather a hypocrite to say that to you, because I do not by any means always do it myself, but I believe we must keep the fourth commandment. If we don't, we're claiming greater wisdom than God. He made us in such a way that we need the rhythm of one day's rest in seven. They tried to change it, you know, during the French Revolution. They tried again in 1917 after the revolution in Russia, but the experiment of trying to make the week of nine or ten days failed. God knew what he was doing when he gave us one day's rest in seven, and we should not claim greater wisdom than he. So these are a few simple thoughts on having time off.

The second item that comes under rest is *hobbies*. While we are young, our hobbies are often sports, and that is excellent for it gives us physical exercise with our friends. But every Christian should have a hobby, even when we are too old to play sports. We ought to take an interest in some branch of natural history, for evangelical Christians have a good doctrine of redemption and a bad doctrine of creation.

I am not ashamed to recommend birdwatching to you. Birdwatchers seldom get nervous breakdowns. Birdwatching takes you into the open air and gets you physical exercise. It takes you away into solitude or semi-solitude with a friend, out of the rush of the city into the quietness of the country-side. I cannot describe the magic of the early morning after sunrise, especially in Africa or Asia, when I've gone out into the bush or into the paddy field to experience the sights and sounds and smells of nature. In addition, it preoccupies the mind, taking it away from the pressures of the office or of your ministry. It also enables you to meditate on the intricacies and the beauties of God's creation. If possible, our hobbies should take us out into the open air.

A third aspect of rest is *time with family and friends.* In our family circle where we know that we are loved and accepted, we can relax, but all of us need friends outside of our family circle as well. Especially we need friends if we are single, and it is good to pray for what the old writers called a 'soul friend', somebody with whom you can share deeply your spiritual experiences. I wonder if we value enough God's good gift of friendship.

I'm going to test your knowledge of Scripture. I'm going to quote a verse to you and I want you to complete it for me. It's written by Paul, from 2 Corinthians 7: 'When we came into Macedonia, this body of ours had no rest, but we were harassed at every turn – conflicts on the outside and fears within. But God, who comforts the downcast, comforted us by . . .' what? How does God comfort us when we are very near breakdown?

Now I'll tell you how superspiritual Christians would fill in the blank. They would write 'God comforted us with the assurance of his love' or 'God comforted us with the presence of Jesus'. But that is not how Paul goes on. He 'comforted us by the coming of Titus', with the arrival of a close friend and the news that he brought. God uses this very human need of friendship to comfort us.

Let me remind you of another example from Paul. This is in his final letter of 2 Timothy. He seems now to have been in a real prison. Many think it was the Mamertine Prison in Rome, which had no windows but only a circle in the ceiling for ventilation and light. Paul was not going to escape from that prison except by execution. He wrote, 'I have fought the good fight, I have finished the race, I have kept the faith' (4:7). Here is Paul in the greatness of his maturity at the end of his life, and yet he was lonely. He was a great, mature Christian, but he was lonely. He writes about the presence of the Lord in 2 Timothy 4:17, 'the Lord stood at my side and gave me strength', and he writes of the expectation of the second coming of Jesus, but neither of these satisfied his loneliness.

Then he writes to Timothy in verse 9, 'Do your best to come to me quickly', and in verse 21, 'Do your best to get here before winter.' Also Paul asks him to bring his cloak that he'd left behind because he was cold, and the scrolls and the parchments, whatever they were. Thus Paul was a great Christian but a very human person, and he was not afraid to admit his need of friends.

So there are three thoughts for you about the discipline of rest and relaxation. There is a need for adequate time off, the need for hobbies or sports, and the need for families and friends. These are human needs. Don't ever be ashamed to admit that we have them.

The discipline of time

Now I would like to go secondly to the discipline of time. I think you know Ephesians 5:16: 'Redeeming the time, because the days are evil' (KJV). Time is a very precious commodity. We all have the same amount of it: sixty minutes in every hour and twenty-four hours in every day. However, some make the most of the time they have, and others don't. Let me say two things under the heading of the discipline of time.

These are human needs. Don't ever be ashamed to admit that we have them.

First is about our daily timetable. Christian leaders and pastors don't usually have an official routine for each day. We don't have a framework of time that is the same every day, so we have to construct our daily timetable, and each day it may be different. Personally, I find it helpful to make a list of what needs to be done and to try to put these tasks for the day into a priority order. I try to allot to each task the time I think it will take in which to do it.

In the morning I find it a great help to pray through the day as it unfolds in the future. If you make a habit of doing that, you will never forget an appointment. When somebody forgets an appointment with me, I always say, 'What were you praying about this morning?'

I find it a great help to pray through the day as it begins; then we face what is coming to us on our knees. It may be a heavy responsibility which we would prefer not to bear. It may be a person we're going to meet for whom we pray before we meet them. I find problems are greatly lessened if you face them in prayer before the day begins.

It seems to be a good thing to get up early if we possibly can. Dr Martyn Lloyd-Jones told me once that it was a question of blood pressure. Some people wake fresh and become progressively more tired during the day. Others wake tired and become progressively fresher during the day. They're not at their best until two o'clock the next morning. I find those people intolerable because my blood pressure is the opposite. I go to bed very tired, but I wake fresh. I find it is wonderful to have two or three hours before breakfast, undisturbed by telephone, by the mail, by callers or by the family. But I recognize that we are different and we must not copy one another.

We must make some time every day for our Bible reading and prayer, and I hope we will make some time each day for reading. Let me share with you a realistic goal. There are too many pastors who never do any reading. That goal is too low. There are also seminaries that recommend that we must spend every morning in study. That goal is too high. We need a realistic goal, and I say to pastors that every pastor could manage one hour of reading a day. In addition, we ought to manage a morning, afternoon or evening every week, that is to say, a longer period of about four hours. One hour a day and one session a week is about ten hours in the week. We ought to be able to manage one book in ten hours, and one book a week is fifty or more a year. I really think that is a reasonable target to set for oneself. These are my only recommendations about the daily timetable.

Now secondly, let me say something about quiet days, and please forgive me if I speak a little about myself. I was appointed rector of All Souls Church in London in 1950. I was only twenty-nine years old. It was a responsibility far beyond my ability and painfully beyond my experience. The responsibilities soon got on top of me and crushed me. Events would arise that I had forgotten to prepare for; an example might have been a special service for which I had forgotten to get the service paper printed. Then I started having the 'preacher's nightmare': I was halfway up the pulpit step and suddenly remembered I had forgotten to prepare a sermon. I suppose in those days I was not far from a breakdown.

Then one day I went to a conference for pastors. There were several speakers, and one speaker made a very simple suggestion. It is the only thing I remember from that conference, and I think I can honestly say it saved my life.

He said every busy pastor should take a quiet day each month. He should go away from his home and his church, and seek to be drawn up into the mind of God and to look forward into the next few months to see where he's going.

It was the word of God to me. I went home and immediately marked the day once a month throughout the year. I put a little 'q' for quiet, and I asked a friend a few miles out of the centre of London if I could come and spend my day in their home. I would spend the whole day there. Nobody knew where I was except my secretary for an emergency. I kept for my monthly quiet day anything that needed time and quiet and prayer: difficult letters to answer, problems to think through, an article to write, the planning of the next three to six months. All I can say is that the burden immediately lifted from me and I hardly ever had the preacher's nightmare again. So valuable did my monthly quiet day become that for ten to fifteen years I made it a weekly quiet day. I very much recommend at least a monthly one to you, especially for more distant planning.

The discipline of devotions

So we've thought of the discipline of rest and relaxation and of the discipline of time. Thirdly, let me say a few things about the discipline of devotions. I'd like to say something about Bible reading and prayer.

First, Bible reading. Christian leaders need to know the whole of the Scriptures. Most misinterpretation of the Bible is due to partial knowledge or to a selective use of the

Bible. The safest of all hermeneutical principles is to know the whole of the Scriptures. Then we learn to interpret each text in the light of all, and the part in the light of the whole.

It was Dr Lloyd-Jones again who many years ago introduced me to a particular Bible reading calendar. I do not necessarily recommend it to you, but I want to tell you about it. My copy is just a very simple calendar. It has been published by different people at different times, but this one is called 'Daily Bread: A Bible Reading Calendar'. It was written by Scottish minister Robert Murray McCheyne in 1842 in order to persuade his people to read the whole Bible through every year. He wanted them to read the New Testament twice and the Old Testament once in order to absorb the whole of the Bible. It is quite a taxing discipline because it involves reading four chapters a day, but this I think is the major value of it. On January 1 we do not begin with Genesis 1 – 4, and January 2 with Genesis 5 – 9. Instead, on the first day of the year, we begin with the four great beginnings of Scripture: Genesis 1, Ezra 1, Matthew 1 and Acts 1. Each is a birth. Genesis 1 is the birth of the universe, Ezra 1 is the rebirth of the nation after the Babylonian exile, Matthew 1 is the birth of Jesus, and Acts 1 is the birth of the Christian church. So we start with the four great beginnings and then follow them through in the year. Nothing has helped me more to trace the themes of Scripture, and light is thrown on one passage of Scripture by another. My practice is to read three chapters in the morning and one in the evening. In the morning I try to read just two and study the third. Of course, just the reading of three chapters would not take more than a quarter of an hour, so we need some study in addition to this general reading.

How can we keep our Bible reading fresh and prevent it from becoming a stale and dull routine? I think my major answer is to come to it with expectation. We should not begin to read without a few minutes of recollection. We need to remind ourselves that God speaks through what he has spoken, and he's more anxious and willing to speak than we are to listen. But the purpose of Bible reading is to listen to the living voice of God, and we need to come to our reading with that living expectation.

Now let me say something about prayer. I guess we all find it difficult, and especially the problem of concentration. Have you ever thought of this strange paradox? On those occasions when we are granted access to God and know that we are in communion with him, nothing is more deeply satisfying to us. The clock stands still, we are in no hurry to stop, we know that this is reality and that we have come home to our Heavenly Father. It may not happen very often, but I hope and believe you have all experienced it sometime and that along with me you have found it most deeply satisfying.

That being so, you would expect us to want to pray. That, however, brings me to the other part of the paradox: that when our prayer time comes around, a strange disinclination to pray descends upon us. A hundred and one innocent alternatives present themselves to our minds: another letter to write, another chapter of the book to read, another programme on television to watch. What is the reason for this illogical paradox? I have no explanation for that paradox except the devil. The devil knows that prayer is the major secret of Christian living, and he is determined to stop us praying if he can. That is the only explanation I can find for this disinclination to pray.

I would like to share with you something that I have found helpful. We need to win what I like to call 'the battle of the threshold'. I sometimes imagine a very high stone wall and the living God is on the other side of the wall. In this walled garden he is waiting for me to come to him. It does seem a rather childish contrivance, but it helps me. There is only one way through the wall into the garden, a tiny little door. Outside the door stands the devil with a drawn sword, ready to contest every inch of the way and to stop me getting through into the presence of God. Now it is at that point that we need to defeat the devil in the name of Christ, and that is the battle of the threshold. I think there are many of us who give up praying before we have won the battle of the threshold. The best way to win this in my experience is claiming the promises of Scripture.

I will give you one example. Funnily enough, it's another Australian example. But it is in Melbourne, not Sydney. This was also in 1958. I'd been invited to lead a mission, both in the University of Sydney and in the University of Melbourne. The Sydney one came first, and I told you how I lost my voice at the end. I was exhausted when that mission was over. Then I had to face a second mission, and I felt like nothing seemed less attractive to me than having to do another mission. I really wanted to take the next flight home. I'd had enough. Now I know it was partly physical and I should have had a holiday, but it was also a spiritual battle. I wasn't excited about the gospel, and I felt as if the Lord had abandoned me.

I was staying in the home of a Christian family. It was the day before the mission began, and I'd locked myself into my bedroom to be alone with the Lord. I knew that I could not begin this mission unless and until I was restored to communion with him. I was reading a number of passages of Scripture, and God chose to use one particular verse to help me. It is Psalm 145:18:

> The Lord is near to all who call on him,
>   to all who call on him in truth.

I can tell you that after a time the load was lifted from me and the Lord made himself known to me again. I went into the mission refreshed and confident, and the Lord blessed.

So I recommend self-discipline in these areas of rest and relaxation, use of time, and devotions, and trust that the Lord will bless richly your life with him.

*Human worth
is intrinsic.*

Chapter 3

THE CHALLENGE OF RELATIONSHIPS

How to treat people with respect

One missionary recruit was asked how he was getting on. He had only been in his new country for a few months. He said he was getting on fine, and he only had two problems. The first was that he couldn't stand his fellow missionaries, and the second was that he couldn't get along with the national Christians. But otherwise everything was fine!

Our third challenge of Christian leadership is the problem of relationships, or how to treat people with respect. It's hard to say enough to emphasize the importance of relationships. Life on earth consists of relationships. There is usually a complex network of relationships. 'None of us lives to himself alone,' said the apostle Paul (Romans 14:7). 'No man is an island,' said a later Christian. There are family and friends, our colleagues, those we serve, the great people who serve us, and they all have claims on us. It is really important that we learn to propagate good relationships.

Respect based on worth: creation and redemption

My first section is the basis for Christians for good relationships. I want to suggest that the basis for good relationships is respect, and respect is based on worth. However, we have to have a Christian understanding of worth. Human worth is not measured by a person's profession or income, or by their good looks or their pleasant personality, or by the size of their house or their car, or by their social status. Human worth is intrinsic.

Here is a basic difference between the Christian mind and the secular mind. Many secular humanists are dedicated to the service of human beings, and sometimes their compassion puts us to shame. However, if you ask them why they want to save human beings, they usually cannot answer except to mutter something about the future of the human race. But there is no basis for caring for the unintelligent or the disabled or the senile if evolutionary potential were the criterion. The logical thing to do then would be to kill people like that lest they hinder the progress of evolution. Secular humanists do not usually reach that conclusion, though, because their hearts are better than

Human worth is intrinsic.

their heads and their philanthropy is better than their philosophy.

But Christians have a better basis for serving human beings. It is not because of what they may become in millions of years in the future, but because of what they already are: not evolution but creation. Creation is the first origin of human worth, and the second is redemption.

Let's look at a verse that has been very helpful to me: Acts 20:28. It's in the middle of the famous speech of Paul's given to the Ephesian elders at Miletus: 'Keep watch over yourselves and all the flock of which the Holy Spirit has made you overseers. Be shepherds of the church of God, which he bought with his own blood.' Notice the reference to the Trinity in that verse, because the basis of pastors' care for their people is a trinitarian basis. They are the shepherds of the church of God. The manuscripts differ; some say 'God', some say 'the Lord'. But I think the correct one is 'the church of God, which he hath purchased with his own blood' (KJV). Some translations read 'with the blood of his own'. That has to be the Son. In any case, it's a reference to the blood itself. So the church of God is purchased with the blood of Christ, but it is the Holy Spirit who has made them guardians of this church. That is a great help to me as a pastor. The Father, the Son and the Holy Spirit are all committed to the welfare of these people, so it is a privilege for me to be involved in their service too. I think we need to keep reminding ourselves who these people are that we are called to serve.

With some hesitation, I would like to share something from my own life. There are times when I've found some people in our church in London to be a great trial and tribulation. After the church service or meeting, I can see them out of the corner of my eye lining up to speak to me. I can tell you that I am tempted to be rude to them and either to tell them to go away or to run away myself.

Honestly, this is the verse that helped me to cope with them. As I speak out loud to them, I am also speaking to them silently in my heart. This is what I'm saying to them silently: 'You may not be much according to some of the world's standards, but you are very precious to God. He made you in his own image. Christ loves you and died for you, and it is a privilege for me to serve you because of your worth.' I find I can laugh about it, but I am also serious because it changes my attitude. Instead of finding them merely amusing, I find I can love and care for them. Thus the basis of good relationships is human worth.

'In the name of the Lord . . . as working for the Lord'

Secondly, I would like to share with you a revolutionary principle in good relationships, and this time I ask you to turn to Colossians 3:17, 23: 'And whatever you do, whether in word or deed, do it all in the name of the Lord Jesus, giving thanks to God the Father through him.' 'Whatever you do, work at it with all your heart, as working for the Lord, not for men.' Notice that both verses begin with the same words: 'whatever you do'. Here are principles of universal application, and they are beautifully complementary to one another. Verse 17 speaks of doing things in the name of the Lord Jesus, and to do something in his name is to do it as his representative or as his proxy. But verse 23 speaks rather of doing things under the Lord Jesus, which means to do things as his servant.

According to the first verse, I'm to treat my neighbour as if I were Jesus Christ, but according to the second I'm to treat my neighbour as if he were Jesus Christ. When I behave to somebody in the name of the Lord, I'm to give him the respect and the courtesy which Jesus Christ would give him. But according to the second verse, I'm to give him the respect and the courtesy which I would give to Jesus Christ. So in any relationship, Jesus Christ is in both people. I can treat you as if I were Christ, and I can treat you as if you were Christ. Either of them is revolutionary, and the two together are doubly revolutionary. Let's look at them both briefly.

The question in every situation is: 'What would Jesus do?'

First, to behave towards people in the name of Christ: in this case we represent Jesus. We are his ambassadors on earth, we learn to think about people as he thought about them, and we learn to treat people as he treated them. We honour women as he honoured them. We love little children as he did. We show compassion to those in need as he did, and we humble ourselves to wash feet as he did. The question in every situation is: 'What would Jesus do?'

There's an American book by Charles Sheldon called *In His Steps*. The story belongs to the late nineteenth century. It was Friday morning, and the pastor was sitting in his study preparing his sermon. His text was 1 Peter 2:21: 'Christ suffered for you, leaving you an example, that you should follow in his steps.' So he was preparing a sermon about following in the steps of Jesus, when suddenly there was a ring at the front doorbell. The pastor looked out of the window and there was a tramp, what you call a 'bum' in America, I think, obviously unemployed. Then the front doorbell rang again. When the pastor went down to talk to the man, the tramp told him a long story about his suffering and unemployment. I forget if the pastor gave him some money, but at least he sent him away as soon as he could and went back to preparing his sermon.

Sunday came and the pastor gave a brilliant and eloquent sermon. But just as he finished, to his great dismay, there was a disturbance at the back of the church. Somebody came walking up the centre aisle, and to his horror it was this tramp. When the tramp got to the front, he turned around and addressed the congregation. He said, 'I was wondering as I sat there in the gallery if what you call following Jesus is the same thing as what he taught.' He went on to tell his story, and he ended, 'What do you Christians mean by following the steps of Jesus?' At that point he fainted for lack of food. The pastor went down from the pulpit in amazement and brought him to his own house, but a few days later the man died. You can understand that this experience revolutionized the congregation.

It was the next Sunday when the pastor challenged the people as to how many of them would enter into a covenant with him that they would not do anything without first asking the question, 'What would Jesus do?' The rest of the book is the story of what happened to different people. Part of the book may be a little sentimental, but he makes the point quite strongly that whatever we do, we are to do it in the name of the Lord Jesus as his representative.

Now we come to the opposite principle, which is to do everything as unto the Lord. This is verse 23. It is in the middle of the instructions to the slaves. They were to be obedient and hardworking, conscientious and honest. Why? Because they were to look behind and beyond their earthly masters and they were to see their heavenly Master and to do everything as unto him and not unto people. In serving their heavenly Lord, they would serve their earthly lord all the better. In this second principle the roles are reversed. The respect and honour we should give people are now not those which Christ would give, but those that Christ would get. Isn't this what Jesus meant about the ministry of love to the hungry and thirsty, the sick and the naked, the strangers and the prisoners? 'In as much as you did it unto one of the least of these, you did it to me.'

This is the principle that we can apply to everything we do. It's possible to clean a room as if we were expecting a visit from Jesus Christ. It's possible to cook a meal as if we were Martha and Jesus were going to eat with us. It's possible to serve the student as if he were Christ. It's possible to write a letter as if Christ were going to read it. It's possible to visit a home as if Jesus lived there. Let me give you one or two other quick examples.

There was a Methodist leader in Britain around the end of the nineteenth century named Samuel Chadwick, and he tells us of his conversion as a boy of ten. It was the Sunday school anniversary, and the visiting preacher happened to say something which struck this little boy. He said that if he were a shiner of shoes, he would be the best shiner of shoes in the village, because he would shine them as if Jesus Christ were going to wear them. That touched that little boy because it was his job at home to clean his father's shoes, and to him it was the most unpleasant job he was given to do.

On Monday morning he began to clean his father's shoes. He began with the rubber boots on the principle that it's best to get the worst over first. But when he'd finished, the preacher's words happened to come to his mind, and he looked at the boots that he'd cleaned. He asked himself whether they would look well on the feet of Jesus Christ. For an answer, he picked them up and cleaned them a second time. He reckons that's the most important thing he ever did in his life. He learned to do everything as unto the Lord.

If I may say so, I think Mother Teresa is a wonderful modern example. I have visited her hospital in Calcutta. I wonder if you know what is written on the board where these Christians work. It is the motto of the Sisters of Charity, and they're Mother Teresa's own words: 'Let each sister see Jesus Christ in the person of the poor. The more repugnant the work or the person, the greater answer must be her faith and love in ministering to our Lord in this distressing disguise.' I love that phrase 'in this distressing disguise'. And with Mother Teresa this was customary. She once said to a visitor, 'I see Christ in every person I touch, because he has said, "I was hungry, thirsty, naked, sick." It is as simple as that. Every time I give a piece of bread, I give it to him.'

Thus, the revolutionary principle I'm talking about is to introduce Christ at both ends of the relationship. On the one hand, we serve in the name of Christ as if we were Christ, and on the other, we serve for the sake of Christ as if those we serve were Christ and we were serving him.

Respect in listening

Could I finish thirdly with some examples of respect? The first has to do with individuals and the need to listen to people. To shut somebody up, to tell somebody to shut up and refuse to listen to him or her, is to treat that person with great disrespect, but to listen to somebody is to express our sense of their worth. There's a lot in the Bible about listening. 'The way of a fool seems right to him, but a wise man listens to advice' (Proverbs 12:15), and 'Everyone should be quick to listen, slow to speak' (James 1:19).

I had a very important experience some years ago. I was still the rector of All Souls Church. Those were the years when we had built up a pastoral team, and we had every Monday morning for a staff meeting. We read the Scriptures and prayed together, and then we would discuss the work of the church and go through the coming week together. On one occasion we were discussing something of import-ance. It was a sharp discussion, and in the middle of it one of my colleagues interrupted, and he turned to me and said, 'John, you're not listening.' He was completely right; I wasn't listening. I had found the discussion a little boring, and I confess that my mind had gone on ahead to something else. That challenge from one of my colleagues was very important in my life, and from that time on I've sought the grace of God to listen. I believe that our relationships deteriorate when we don't listen to one another.

Let me give you three points about listening. First, *listening is right* in itself because it is respectful. Second, *listening is therapeutic*. It gives the person who is speaking the opportunity to put their trouble into words, and when you put your problem into words you automatically diminish it. Our problems are at their worst when they lurk in the dark corners of our hearts, but when we bring them out and articulate them and look at them, they immediately become smaller. Therefore, listening to somebody who is bringing out their problems is therapeutic to that person.

Third, *listening is productive*, especially if we are listening to people with whom we disagree. People who disagree with one another usually avoid one another. They keep apart, and then they write books against one another and lob hand grenades at one another across no-man's-land. Then a grotesque image of that person develops in my mind, and I can clearly see his image, his horns and hoof and tail. This develops within my mind when he is thousands of miles away. But once we have the courage to meet one another and look one another in the face and listen to one another, we discover to our surprise that he is a human being. And not only a human being but a brother or sister in the Lord, and even reasonable!

I've had a number of examples of this in international consultations. Let me tell you about a consultation on the relationship between evangelism and social action. There has been a fierce debate between those who believe that the mission of their church is only evangelistic and those who believe that evangelism and social action belong together in the mission of the church. Some of you know Arthur Johnston's book called *The Battle for World Evangelism*, and I can sum up its thesis in about three sentences. The World Council of Churches began with great evangelistic zeal in 1910, but has gradually lost its evangelistic impetus ever since. This historical analysis is accurate and helpful. The second point is that the Lausanne movement is going in the same direction. It is becoming liberal on the Bible and it is embracing the social gospel. His third point was this: the villain of the piece is a man called Stott.

Arthur Johnston and I are now good friends, but he had written part of this book against me. I then wrote an open letter to Arthur Johnston, which the editor of *Christianity Today* agreed to publish, so there we are writing against one another. Afterwards, however, I wrote to Art Johnston and suggested that we could have a consultation about it and meet face to face. He and I could both be on the planning committee, and we would both ensure that our two points of view were adequately represented.

That is what happened when we met in Grand Rapids. When I arrived, I was nearly in despair because a number of synopses had been circulated in advance. The disagreement was very sharp, and some of the papers were rude and even shrill in their criticism. I wondered if we could ever come to any degree of agreement.

For the first three days we made no progress, as people had to get their convictions off their chests, but gradually we began to listen to one another. Listen carefully to this: we not only listened to what people were saying, but we listened to what was behind what they were saying, what were their real concerns and what it was that they were really anxious to safeguard. Then we found to our surprise that we wanted to safeguard it too. Once we had really listened to one other, there was hope. The result was a document about the relationship between evangelism and social action. It doesn't express a total agreement, but it expresses a very substantial agreement.

Respect in decision-making

One final thing. I move from listening to decision-making. This has to do more with groups than with individuals. Once again the Christian mind and the secular mind are different from each other. We Christians assume too rigidly that we can simply take over secular methods of decision-making. In the secular democratic process, decisions are made by simple majority: fifty-one for, fifty against, and the motion is won. There are many churches and church bodies that make decisions in the same way, but I'm certain that the Holy Spirit is grieved by it. To make decisions by simple majority vote is a sign of no confidence in the Holy Spirit, and a regretful lack of respect for the minority. The Holy Spirit is a spirit of truth and of love, and we, the Christian mind, should surely look for substantial agreement.

I will finish with one more example, if I may, from my experience. This is again going back many years. Our church council would go away for a complete day every year. We would keep for our day conference important matters of debate. This particular year the major project was whether we would use modern language in church services. Would we continue to address God as 'thee' and 'thou' or permit 'you'? I was personally convinced that we needed to move into modern language, but there were a number of older members of the congregation who loved the beauty of the Elizabethan English.

There was a sharp debate, and it was evident that the council was almost equally divided. We could have settled it by vote, but we had decided not to use that method of decision-making. 'So,' I said at the end of the day, 'let us leave the matter as it is. We will wait a whole year. We will think further about the matter. We will pray about it. If any of you wishes to circulate a memorandum about your convictions, feel free to do so.'

Well, the next year arrived. I can remember very well leaving my study before I went to the day conference, and

I said to the Lord, 'If all you can give me is one evening a month [to use the modern language], I will accept that.' We had a further discussion, and I am telling you the truth, the decision was unanimous to have modern English every Sunday evening. And we have never gone back. Again it was a wonderful example for me of the need to listen to one another, to respect one another, to expect the Holy Spirit to lead us to a common mind, and to give him time in which to do so.

Christian leaders know that the Lord is the one who trains, nourishes and accompanies them.

Chapter 4

THE CHALLENGE
OF YOUTH

How to be a leader when comparatively young

It's hard to be a leader when comparatively young. I do not regard myself as young, but youth is a period of great joy and privilege. When we are young, we are strong and energetic. We have confidence and enthusiasm. It's great to be young. At the same time, it can be extremely frustrating. The older generation does not always trust young people. They often treat them as if they were still kids. They don't easily accept them as adults in their own right, and they find it difficult to accept them as leaders. Thus, young people often get irritated and frustrated. What can they do?

Let's study a passage of Scripture and learn some lessons from Timothy. Paul writes in 1 Timothy 4:11 – 5:5:

Command and teach these things. Don't let anyone look down on you because you are young, but set an example for the believers in speech, in life, in love, in faith and in purity. Until I come, devote yourself to the public reading of Scripture, to preaching and to teaching. Do not neglect your gift, which was given you through a prophetic message when the body of elders laid their hands on you.

Be diligent in these matters; give yourself wholly to them, so that everyone may see your progress. Watch your life and doctrine closely. Persevere in them, because if you do, you will save both yourself and your hearers.

Do not rebuke an older man harshly, but exhort him as if he were your father. Treat younger men as brothers, older women as mothers, and younger women as sisters, with absolute purity.

Let's look again at verses 11 and 12: 'Command and teach these things. Don't let anyone look down on you because you are young.' I think the tension is clearly seen in both verses. On the one hand, Timothy has been put in the position of authority. He was the apostle Paul's delegate or representative in Corinth, and therefore it was his job to command and teach these things. In other words, he was to pass on to the church at Ephesus the doctrines and duties of the apostle Paul, so there was his authority.

On the other hand, he was still a relatively young man. The Greek word for *youth* was used to describe people at least until the age of forty. Probably Timothy was still in his thirties, and compared with some of the elders in the church he may have seemed very young. There was a real danger that some would despise his youth and reject his ministry. Perhaps some of the elders were resentful that he had been promoted over their heads. They may have rejected his authority because of his youth and rejected his ministry because he was inexperienced.

Perhaps you can see yourself in his position. How should young leaders react if their ministry is being rejected or resented? Not by anger or resentment. Not by becoming aggressive or oppressing themselves. But, and this is a strong adversative in the Greek, Paul spells out an alternative way. J. B. Phillips put it quite well: 'Don't let people look down on you because you are young; see that they look up to you because you are an example to them in your speech and behaviour, in your love and faith and sincerity.'

Watch your example

Paul gives Timothy six words of advice. First, *watch your example*. Verse 12, set an example. If Timothy wanted his leadership to be accepted, he must set a good example. They would not despise his youth if they could admire his life. Setting an example is the new style of leadership that Jesus introduced into the world. It is leadership by example instead of by autocracy. When our authority is questioned, threatened or resisted, the great temptation is to insist more strongly, but we have to resist that temptation.

Notice how comprehensive his example and model are to be: in speech and life, in love and faith and purity. Perhaps that is the hardest: faith in God, and self-control.

It would be hard to exaggerate the disastrous consequences of a bad example or the beneficial influences of a good one. So the first advice to a young leader is: watch your example.

Identify your authority

Second, *identify your authority*. In verse 13 Paul says, 'Until I come'. Those words express his self-conscious, apostolic authority. When he was personally present in Ephesus, he would exercise authority. He would be the teacher of doctrine and ethics. He would settle disputes and administer discipline. So the question was what was to happen when he was absent. Timothy, however, was not an apostle, so how should he behave?

Paul says, 'Until I come, devote yourself to the public reading of Scripture.' Some versions simply say, 'Devote yourself to reading', but the Greek verb for reading is *anagnosis*, which is always used as public reading either of a petition, of a will or from the pulpit. What document was Timothy to read publicly? Well, certainly the Old Testament Scriptures. *Anagnosis* is used of Ezra's reading of the law, and also in Nehemiah 8:8, and it is used of Jesus' reading of Isaiah in the Nazareth synagogue. In the synagogue services, the Law and the Prophets were always read.

But surely Paul is not only referring to the Old Testament Scriptures. He must have been referring to his own letters and the letters of the other apostles, for in other places he directly says his message should be read publicly. See these references: 1 Thessalonians 5:27, 'I charge you before the

Lord to have this letter read to all the brothers.' Colossians 4:16, 'After this letter has been read to you, see that it is also read in the church of the Laodiceans.' Revelation 1:3, 'Blessed is the one who reads the words of this prophecy.' In the Christian assemblies there would be two public readings: not the Law and the Prophets as in the synagogues, but the Old Testament on the one hand and the apostles' letters and memoirs on the other. Of course, that is the origin of our having an Old and a New Testament lesson in church today. Each local church began to make its own collection of these authoritative Christian writings.

But there was something else that Timothy was to do. He was not only to read the Scriptures, but to preach and teach out of them. Preaching and teaching are literally exhortation and instruction. Now it was already a custom in the synagogue. First there was the reading and then the instruction or exhortation of it, and the practice was taken over into the Christian assembly. This is what Timothy was to do in the absence of the apostle, and in the absence of the apostle, we must do the same when we read that from the Scriptures. We are identifying our authority. The careful exegesis of Scripture is essential for the young leader, so first watch your example and second identify your authority.

Exercise your gifts

Thirdly, *exercise your gifts*. Verse 14, 'Do not neglect your gift, which was given you through a prophetic message when the body of elders laid their hands on you.' The reference seems to be to what we would call Timothy's ordination, at which the elders laid their hands on him, the prophetic office was given, and at the same time a spiritual gift was bestowed on Timothy. The Greek word there is *charisma*. We're not told what that *charisma* was, but clearly it was some kind of ordination gift, perhaps the authority to preach together with the power of the Spirit equipping him to do so. This gift for ministry Timothy must not neglect, but rather he must kindle it, as Paul writes in 2 Timothy 1:6.

So, Timothy had to remember that God had called him to his ministry and gifted him for it, and that the church had recognized his call and gifts by the laying on of hands. If he would exercise his gifts and ministry, people would not despise his youth. All spiritual gifts are gifts for ministry, and people are not likely to reject our ministry if they can see our gifts, because then they have to concede that God has gifted us for the ministry.

Share your progress

The fourth piece of advice: *share your progress*. Verse 15, 'Be diligent in these matters, give yourself wholly to them, so that everyone may see your progress.' So far Paul has referred to Timothy's example, authority, commission and gifts. Now he says, 'Be diligent in these matters and devote yourself, hold yourself wholly to them, because if you do that, people will see your progress.'

Timothy was not only to be conscientious; he was also to show improvement in his ministry. He was to grow in spiritual maturity and ministry. People were to see not only what he was, but what he was becoming. I think that's very important for young leaders, because sometimes leaders are put on a pedestal and then they are supposed to be perfect. But this is dishonest in itself, and it's very discouraging for other people. Instead, we are to echo what Paul says: 'Not that I have already obtained it or have already become perfect' (Philippians 3:12 NASB). So let it be seen that we are making progress.

Mind your consistency

Now the fifth bit of advice: *mind your consistency*. Verse 16, 'Watch your life and doctrine closely. Persevere in them, because if you do, you will save both yourself and your hearers.' It is important to see how Paul links his life and his teaching. Literally, he must pay close attention both to himself and to his doctrine. That combination is significant. He was neither to neglect himself in teaching others nor was he to neglect others in being concerned with himself. He was to practise what he preached and to apply his teaching to himself and others equally. Balanced Christian leadership demands that we persevere in both.

Then we will save both ourselves and others. Paul has not lost his reason and begun to preach self-salvation. He is simply warning that faith without works is dead, and it's no good our teaching other people if we don't practise what we preach.

Adjust your relationships

That leads me to the sixth piece of advice: *adjust your relationships*. From the evidence of 1 Timothy 5:1–2 it is clear that the congregation that Timothy was responsible for was mixed. It was mixed in sex, both male and female, and it was mixed in age, both old and young. So the age and sex of people should determine Timothy's attitude towards them. Take the older people first. Timothy might have to admonish people much older than himself. If so, he must do it as an exhortation and not as a rebuke: 'Do not rebuke an older man harshly, but exhort him as if he were your father.' The senior members were to be given respect due to age and the affection due to parents. In other words, he was to treat older men as fathers and older women as mothers.

I am often called 'Uncle John', and there is a good theological reason for this. This is my scriptural warrant. I genuinely believe that we should recognize the generation gap in the Christian community. Sometimes students in London come up to me and call me 'John', even when I do not know who they are, and even if I am older than their father or in some cases their grandfather! I think that is unnatural. Of course, I recognize that there is a cultural element here, but in the cultures of Africa and Asia, a young person would never dream of calling an older one by his first name, and the young people always call the older ones 'uncle'.

Let us take Timothy's own generation. He was to treat the younger men as brothers, that is, loving them and not talking down to them, and he was to treat the younger women as sisters, loving them too but with absolute purity, taking sensible precautions to avoid immorality.

So the local church is a family. In the local church there are fathers and mothers, brothers and sisters. Young Christian leaders must be sensitive to these differences, not treating everybody alike, but treating the elders with respect, their own generation with equality, the opposite sex with restraint and charity, and all of the ages of both sexes with the love that binds the Christian family together.

Let me recapitulate these six pieces of advice, for there is much practical wisdom here for the young leader. One, watch your example, setting the believers a good one. Two, identify your authority, reading and expounding the Scriptures. Three, exercise your gifts, so people see evidence of God's call and equipment. Four, show your progress, so that your spiritual growth is obvious to everybody. Five, mind your consistency, committing no dichotomies between your teaching and your behaviour. Six, adjust your relationships, treating members of the church family according to their age and sex.

If young leaders follow these apostolic instructions, they will be able to command and teach out of the Scripture, as verse 11 says, without finding that their youth is despised or that their ministry is rejected.

The Christian leader has been commissioned by God for a task of responsibility and service. Every leader faces pressures and conflicts that arise from the spiritual battle that Satan is waging against the gospel and those who proclaim it. But Christian leaders know that the Lord is the one who trains, nourishes and accompanies them. If we learn to heed the teachings of our Master, if we obey his commandments, if we follow in his footsteps, then our yoke will be light and we can fulfil our mission effectively and with joy.

Christian leaders know that the Lord is the one who trains, nourishes and accompanies them.

*John introduced me to
the Majority World,
not as an object but
as a family.*

* * * * *

*The centrality of the
cross remained like
a deep subterranean
undercurrent . . .
affecting and directing
so much of his
thinking on ethical,
theological and
pastoral issues.*

Chapter 5

TWO 'TIMOTHYS'

Mark Labberton and Corey Widmer

Mark Labberton and Corey Widmer were two of John Stott's many 'Timothys'. The following reflections are excerpted from *John Stott: A Portrait by His Friends*, edited by Christopher J. H. Wright (Inter-Varsity Press, 2011).

The sermon on the carpet *by Mark Labberton*

The most memorable sermon I heard John Stott preach was not delivered at All Souls or at a large gathering in Asia, Africa or Latin America, or at a church or theological institution. Without a pulpit, surrounded by mud, and standing only on a small piece of carpet honorifically brought forth for him, John preached on this occasion to a handful of people in a dark, dilapidated courtyard, surrounded by small fire pits, blackened pots and a set of simple homes.

This spontaneous sermon occurred as the outcome of a favour asked for by an Anglican priest serving in Burma. 'Would it be possible,' the priest wrote, 'for John Stott to pay a pastoral visit to my elderly mother the next time he is in Madras, India?' Since the man served so far away from his mother, he wondered if John might well not get to her before he could, since she might not have long to live. He added, doubtless for extra motivation, that his mother was poor, declining in health and 'her teeth are falling out one by one'.

On his next visit to Madras, John indeed took the scant information he had, more like the designation of large neighbourhood than a house address, and set off with two of us to find this elderly lady. After a couple of hours searching, passing under and through various layers of shacks and structures, we arrived at the door to the woman's home. She eventually emerged from the shadows, frail, nearly toothless, but smiling with a tearful joy. She knelt at John's feet and kissed them, and then she and John spoke through our translator for a few minutes. She made the request for a word of blessing, and once John had agreed, the carpet was brought forth and John prayed and offered his brief sermon.

The text was John 3:16. The words were simple and clear. The tone was compassionate and dignified. The assurance was personal and tender. The man who typically preached in a spotlight to hundreds and thousands, across a wide range of tribes and tongues and nations, with intellectual rigour and verbal command, now preached amid shadows to one woman and a handful of neighbours.

As his study assistant, accompanying John on this trip to India and Bangladesh, I was privileged with this view of John the highly visible preacher, and John the nearly invisible pastor. What struck me then and now was John's consistency in each role and his faithfulness to Christ in both. John was simply trying to love his neighbour, the priest in Burma, by serving his mother, the widow in India. All John did on that occasion was to fulfil a simple request. But to do so required personal persistence. It meant stepping away from the crowd – the same person, serving the same Lord.

My first exposure to John had occurred when I was twenty-three at IVCF's Urbana Student Missions Convention. The most captivating part of that week for me was the question-and-answer session that John led. Hundreds of people, out of the thousands at Urbana, showed up for this informal Q&A time. I was greatly struck by the humility and clarity of John's responses, by his knowledge of the Bible and by his self-effacing humour.

At one point, a theological student asked a very long and technical question, using many multisyllabic theological terms. John asked the young man first to define each of the words he had used, and second to restate his question more simply. It was, frankly, awkward and insistent – maybe even a little embarrassing – for the seminarian. He did as John had asked, however, and then John proceeded to respond to the question simply and clearly. Although I had not yet met John in person, this exchange suggested what I later found to be true of him: a drive for clarity, a confidence in rationality, an expectation of competency. John embodied these, even as he encouraged them in others.

While his demanding capacity and competence were impressive, what moved and intrigued me much more was his character. Who is this man? Is he who he seems to be? How did he become that person? Standing several years later in that darkened courtyard in India, I thought back to that Q&A session at Urbana. The integrity of John's life and ministry was not only apparent on-stage but off-stage as well. The humble and earnest devotion he expressed in public was also evident in private. John has sought to live one life serving one Lord.

Although I was a young Christian and recent seminary graduate at the time I came to work as John's study assistant, it had already become clear to me that while God provides gifts for ministry, the greater effect comes through character, the fruit of God's Spirit. Charisma, winsomeness, popularity, charm and cleverness can matter – in fact, they can matter too much. What endures and bears peculiar witness to God comes from beyond mere capacity before a crowd. The greater testimony comes in an otherwise unexplained character. This is what drew people to Jesus. This is what is meant to be true of Jesus' disciples.

The sermon on the carpet was the most memorable of John's sermons to me because it was the sermon that was John's life. His spiritual gifts might have taken him to

India, to offer a set of lectures, to speak about important things with important leaders. But it was his character that got him into that darkened courtyard. The sermon he offered mattered not because of his degrees or his achievements or his honours, but because he had tasted that the Lord was good and had good news to share with an elderly sister in Christ who was blessed by that encouragement. The circumstances that distinguished John's life from this woman's life were vast. But what they held in common mattered more, and they both knew that.

Over the three decades that I've known John, I have undoubtedly put him through some of the scrutiny that mentors often have to endure. I have wrestled internally with places of agreement and disagreement, with choices made or not, with our differences in attitude or experience, culture or generation. I don't have the same confidence in human reason that John does. I don't share the same rigorous commitment to self-discipline. The spiritual glass through which I look is not as clear as the one through which John sees. All that now seems like mere difference without division. For what still draws me to John more than anything else is the aroma of John's life – a life centred and matured in the love of Jesus Christ that bears fruit to the glory of God. John was all the more impressive, not less, the deeper our relationship became.

What I feared most from my early exposure to the Christian faith was that it seemed to make life smaller rather than larger – less love, less joy, less creativity, less wonder, less engagement. I was exposed to some pastors who seemed to be the incarnational proof that this was so. But when I came to faith in Christ as a young college student, I discovered that Jesus saves us from smallness.

I remembered this in Madras. As John preached that day, I stood so far from where I had been born and raised. I was now working for a pastor whose vision of the gospel had a cosmic and global reach, and who showed me in character and action that to be a disciple of Jesus meant growing in wisdom and love, in humility and hope. The world John knew and served was not parochial. The personal gospel was not a private one, and the particularity of the gospel was for the sake of its universality.

John introduced me to the Majority World, not as an object but as a family.

John introduced me to the Majority World, not as an object but as a family. His heart had grown far beyond his upper-class home and his elite education. He carried daily a vivid sense of the vital faith and strength of brothers and sisters around the world. He prayed daily as one standing alongside a very large family, with its size and urgency making it all the more compelling. I have experienced with peoples from many places and cultures our common centre in Jesus Christ, and the ways our hearts and minds grew towards our Lord because of our brother John.

What John taught me in that sermon in Madras was what his life has taught me over the last thirty years. God so loved the world that the gift of God's Son reorders and enlarges our hearts and our lives. The one gospel of our Lord and Saviour Jesus Christ both intensifies and enlarges our understanding of God, and of the worth of our diverse brothers and sisters in Christ, and of all our earthly neighbours. The God who loves us all takes us where God wants, in order that we might show and proclaim this love for the transformation of the world and for the sake of God's glory. It was clear to me that day as John stood on the carpet in the courtyard: John was simply being himself, the new self that was and is being renewed in the likeness of Jesus.

Mark Labberton was one of John Stott's early study assistants. He went on to be senior pastor at First Presbyterian Church, Berkeley, California. He has served on the board of John Stott Ministries in the United States and is now the president of Fuller Theological Seminary, Pasadena, California.

'Above all, cling to the Cross' *by Corey Widmer*

I have countless memories of my three years serving as Uncle John's study assistant, but two anecdotes are the most prominent in my mind. The first occurred after just a few months in the very mundane pattern of our daily life together. Every morning, at 11 am sharp, I would bring him a cup of coffee. I would find him hunched over some letter or manuscript at his desk, consumed with the work

before him, putting his unparalleled powers of concentration to whatever task was at hand. Not wanting to disturb
him, I would quietly set the cup and saucer adjacent to his
right hand, and oftentimes he would mumble a barely
audible word of thanks: 'I'm not worthy.'

Initially I thought this comment was amusing, but after
a few months I began to find it slightly bothersome. How
could someone pronounce himself unworthy of an acidic
cup of instant coffee? One morning I was feeling a little
cheeky, and when Uncle John mumbled his usual expression, 'I'm not worthy', I quipped back, 'Oh, sure you are.'

Uncle John stopped, and I saw the powerful magnetic
look of his concentration ease from the papers before him.
He slowly raised his gaze, and, with a look of immense
seriousness, yet boyish playfulness, he responded, 'You
haven't got your theology of grace right.' I laughed, grinned
awkwardly, and then said, 'It's only a cup of coffee, Uncle
John.' As I turned round and headed back into the kitchen,
I heard him mutter, 'It's just the thin end of the wedge.'

It took me days to figure out what he meant by that final
rejoinder in our exchange. Though I never discussed it with
him, I am convinced that he meant this: if our commitment
to Jesus Christ and our understanding of his grace do not
impact the small places in our daily lives – the 'thin end of
the wedge' – then we are not living integrated lives. Our
commitment to Christ may be most richly expressed in the
most apparently inconsequential moments.

Uncle John was always fond of talking about 'whole-life
discipleship' – that is, his concern that the comprehensive

lordship of Jesus Christ would extend its reign over every dimension of the Christian's life, bridging the 'sacred-secular' divide that often separates our 'spiritual' lives from our 'secular' commitments and interactions.

I saw this same commitment deeply manifested in his daily life, in the way he carefully negotiated a simple life-style, in his concern for the physical and material environment, in his interactions with taxi drivers, waiters, hotel concierges and other sundry people who crossed his path, and above all in his gentle and winsome engagement with Frances and me on a daily basis. He truly was an 'integrated' Christian, and the grace of the gospel infused even the thinnest ends of the wedge that was his life.

The second anecdote relates to a very different setting: in hot, balmy Madras, India. We were there for a preaching conference in 2002, and one afternoon while birdwatching, Uncle John took a nasty fall over a cement curb and lacerated his right leg. What looked to be a fairly harmless cut (one that would have healed naturally for someone less elderly) soon became a painful, swollen and infected wound, and began to worsen daily. Over two days we visited at least three different doctors in several different hospitals, but no treatment seemed to be halting the wound's deterioration. Finally, I was able to get in touch with Uncle John's cardiologist back in London, and with grave concern in his voice the doctor warned me of the immense seriousness of the situation, in view of the state of Uncle John's heart. He insisted that if things did not improve immediately, we should come back to London as soon as possible.

Later that day, Uncle John and I were together in his room as I recounted to him the concern of his doctor. It was as solemn a moment as I ever shared with him. I believe that both of us perceived that, with the real possibility of serious infection and blood poisoning, these could possibly be his last days on the earth. Despite this fact and the pain that he was experiencing, he remained light-hearted and engaging, as always. Almost as if he recognized that this might well be some of the last time we would share together, he began talking with me about my future, about my desire to be a pastor, about what he considered the most vital dimensions of the pastoral ministry. Of all that he shared with me in those precious moments, one piece of advice has stayed with me more than any other: 'Above all,' he said, 'cling to the cross.'

The centrality of the cross remained like a deep subterranean undercurrent . . . affecting and directing so much of his thinking on ethical, theological and pastoral issues.

The cross of Christ, the title of what he considered his most important book and the one in which he invested more of himself than any other, was the paramount theme, the one he returned to again and again. He took quite literally Paul's call in Galatians 6:14, one of his 'life verses' as he often called it, to be 'obsessed' with the cross. Even when he was not speaking about it directly, the centrality of the cross remained like a deep subterranean undercurrent beneath the body of Uncle John's life and work, affecting and directing so much of his thinking on ethical, theological and pastoral issues. 'The Pervasive Influence of the Cross' is the title of the epilogue of *The Cross of Christ*. It could just as well serve as an epilogue for his life.

Thankfully, Uncle John's leg did heal, and several more years of ministry lay ahead for him beyond that moment in India. Those were not his final words to me, as it turned out. But for me, they endure beyond all others.

Corey Widmer was John Stott's study assistant from 1999 to 2002. Since 2005, he has been associate pastor of outreach at Third Presbyterian Church, Richmond, Virginia, USA, and since 2008, co-pastor of East End Fellowship, a multi-ethnic fellowship.

Appendix

JOHN STOTT ON MINISTRY, LEADERSHIP AND SERVICE

The very first priority

The very first thing which needs to be said about Christian ministers of all kinds is that they are 'under' people (as their servants) rather than 'over' them (as their leaders, let alone their lords). Jesus made this absolutely plain. The chief characteristic of Christian leaders, he insisted, is humility not authority, and gentleness not power.

The Message of 1 & 2 Thessalonians, p. 120

The true model

'Ministry' means 'service' – lowly, menial service; it is, therefore, curiously perverse to turn it into an occasion for boasting. Jesus specifically distinguished between 'rule' and 'service', 'authority' and 'ministry', and added that though the former was characteristic of pagans, the latter was to characterize his followers: 'You know that those who are regarded as rulers of the Gentiles lord it over them, and their high officials exercise authority over them. Not so with you. Instead, whoever wants to become great among you must be your servant, and whoever wants to be first must be slave of all. For even the Son of Man did not come to be served, but to serve, and to give his life as a ransom for many' (Mark 10:42–45). Thus Christian ministers are to take as their model the Christ who came to serve, not the Gentiles (or the Pharisees) who preferred to be lords.

Christ in Conflict, pp. 185–186

Leadership, not lordship

Leadership and lordship are two quite different concepts. The Christian leads by example, not force, and is to be a model who invites a following, not a boss who compels one.

The Message of 1 Timothy & Titus, p. 120

Guardians and heralds

It was Paul's firm assurance that his message came from God, and that 'his' gospel was in reality 'God's' gospel. He had not invented it. He was only a steward entrusted with it and a herald commissioned to proclaim it. He must above all else be faithful.

Every authentic Christian ministry begins here, with the conviction that we have been called to handle God's Word as its guardians and heralds . . . Of course we are not apostles of Christ like Paul. But we believe that in the New Testament the teaching of the apostles has been preserved and is now bequeathed to us in its definitive form. We are therefore trustees of this apostolic faith, which is the Word of God and which works powerfully in those who believe. Our task is to keep it, study it, expound it, apply it and obey it.

The Message of 1 & 2 Thessalonians, p. 68

The beginnings of pastoral oversight

Although no fixed ministerial order is laid down in the New Testament, some form of pastoral oversight (*episkope*), doubtless adapted to local needs, is regarded as indispensable to the welfare of the church. We notice that it was both local and plural – local in that the elders were chosen from within the congregation, not imposed from without, and plural in that the familiar modern pattern of 'one pastor one church' was simply unknown. Instead, there was a pastoral team, which is likely to have included (depending on the size of the church) full-time and part-time ministers, paid and voluntary workers, presbyters, deacons and deaconesses. Their qualifications Paul laid down in writing later. These were mostly matters of moral integrity, but loyalty to the apostles' teaching and a gift for teaching it were also essential. Thus the shepherds would tend Christ's sheep by feeding them, in other words, care for them by teaching them.

The Message of Acts, p. 236

The Christian pastor

The pastor is primarily a teacher. This is the reason for two qualifications for the presbyterate which are singled out in the Pastoral Epistles. First, the candidate must be 'able to teach' (1 Timothy 3:2). Secondly, he must 'hold firmly to the trustworthy message as it has been taught, so that he can encourage others by sound doctrine and refute those who oppose it' (Titus 1:9). These two qualifications go together. Pastors must both be loyal to the apostolic teaching (the *didache*) and have a gift for teaching it (*didaktikos*). And whether they are teaching a crowd or congregation, a group or an individual (Jesus himself taught in all three contexts), what distinguishes their pastoral work is that it is always a ministry of the Word.

The Contemporary Christian, p. 286

An enabling ministry

The New Testament concept of the pastor is not of a person who jealously guards all ministry in his own hands and successfully squashes all lay initiatives, but of one who helps and encourages all God's people to discover, develop and exercise their gifts. His teaching and training are directed to this end, to enable the people of God to be a servant people, ministering actively but humbly according to their gifts in a world of alienation and pain. Thus, instead of monopolizing all ministry himself, he actually multiplies ministries.

The Message of Ephesians, p. 167

The accountability of ministry

No secret of Christian ministry is more important than its fundamental God-centredness. The stewards of the gospel are primarily responsible neither to the church, nor to its synods or leaders, but to God himself. On the one hand, this is a disconcerting fact, because God scrutinizes our hearts and their secrets, and his standards are very high. On the other hand, it is marvellously liberating, since God is a more knowledgeable, impartial and merciful judge than any human being or ecclesiastical court or committee. To be accountable to him is to be delivered from the tyranny of human criticism.

The Message of 1 & 2 Thessalonians, pp. 50–51

Love and service

If love and truth go together, and love and gifts go together, so do love and service, since true love always expresses itself in service. To love is to serve. We are left, then, with these four aspects of Christian life forming a ring or a circle that cannot be broken – love, truth, gifts and service. For love issues in service, service uses the gifts, the highest gift is the teaching of the truth, but truth must be spoken in love. Each involves the others, and wherever you begin, all four are brought into operation. Yet 'the greatest of these is love' (1 Corinthians 13:13).

Baptism and Fullness, p. 151

Most of these excerpts are drawn from *Authentic Christianity: From the Writings of John Stott*, edited by Timothy Dudley-Smith (Inter-Varsity Press, 1995).

For more information about IVP
and our publications visit

www.ivpbooks.com

Get regular updates at **ivpbooks.com/signup**
Find us on **facebook.com/ivpbooks**
Follow us on **twitter.com/ivpbookcentre**

Inter-Varsity Press, a company limited by guarantee registered in England and Wales, number 05202650. Registered office IVP Bookcentre, Norton Street, Nottingham NG7 3HR, United Kingdom. Registered charity number 1105757.